CHANGE YOUR ENERGY, CHANGE YOUR LIFE.

Thoughts on retraining
your way of thinking

DEDICATION

To those in search of themselves…

I hope this guide encourages you to use the gift of positive energy. Use it as a tool to reprogram your mind. Though recreating ourselves can be a great challenge, it is most definitely not impossible to achieve.

To my queens…

Empress Menen, Malaya Symone, and Ja'Sira Vi. My three amazing daughters, you are the reason for my elevation. I love you with all of my existence, for infinity. And to the strongest person I've ever met, my mother, I love you.

To my ancestors…

I say to you, Ase.

TABLE OF CONTENTS

INTRODUCTION

Energy, chakra, change, and balance.

Our lives are a function of our energies. Whatever situation you find yourself in, whatever position you are in, understand that it's mainly because of your energy. We always blame individuals and circumstances for justifying why we are not where we want to be. Sometimes we say it's because of our finances, our relationships, our pessimistic relatives, and so on. Other times, it's because we don't have enough time, maybe too old, or perhaps we are not kind enough. But i assure you, most of the time, the problem is us. Many people never really focus on their energy and how they can manipulate it to change their lives.

The conservation laws tell us that energy, like matter, is neither created nor destroyed but transferred from form to another. This means that energy exists in everything. We, humans, are also made up of energy, and we can move it to other people or things around us. Energy will flow in both a conscious and unconscious state.

"It's all energy, and that's all there is to it. Balance the magnitude of your preferred reality, and you can't help but get the reality. It could not be any other way. It's not philosophy. This is physics."

Albert Einstein presented a new understanding of nature concerning energy with these terms. Spirituality and science have been considered two entirely unrelated disciplines for many decades now as if they have little in common. However, the best and effective way to understand both of them and put them to use in our lives is to see and treat them as one.

Energy in itself is pure, and it flows from one vessel to another, but the form in which it is transmitted differs. It affects people differently, thereby changing or altering their lives. For example, in the form of electricity, energy is compatible with electronics. When energy is supplied to the electronics, they will function. However, that same electric energy, if not moderated, can damage the same electronic device it was compatible with initially. Energy in the form of electricity can cause a lot of harm. Human energy is more than the scope of calories we gain from eating carbs and fatty food. A high protein or carb diet does not affect how you feel about your day, but what someone said or did to you yesterday may affect you temporarily or permanently.

Change can bring about growth and improvement. Finding yourself in this modern society that keeps changing requires a similar response from you to ensure your survival. As people, even if we may not need much effort to adjust to physical phenomena like climate change, natural disasters, etc. However, we need many attempts when dealing with other ever-changing energy around us. Effecting this change is not as easy as putting on a sweater when you feel cold or tak that's around us. Effecting this change is not as easy as putting on a sweater when you feel cold or taking a bite when you are hungry. It focuses more on evaluating ourselves personally to identify aspects of our lives that need change and taking steps to make the changes. These changes are usually made at a systematic level, where we have already created automatic responses to different forms of energies we have been encountering in our lives. By making such changes, we change our energies and, thus, our lives.

Inner energy is quite different from most physical forms like steam, nuclear, hydro, electric, etc. How we manipulate that internal energy becomes the next question to change our lives. We do that by learning and understanding this energy through spirituality and self-discipline. The spiritual aspect deals with the various ways we can access and amplify our energy, and it involves concepts like mindfulness and chakra techniques. The self-preparation and discipline aspect deals with preparing yourself for the new energy levels you want to unlock for the new person you want to be.

The chakras are meridian spots in their very core, which represent different types of energy within your specific field of energy. Chakras are an incredibly unique model that precisely defines the circulation of spiritual energy within an individual's spiritual and physical bodies. Although each person essentially has 114 chakras and thousands of chakras outside their bodies, we usually only talk about working with the seven primary chakras within the body system when we talk about working with chakras.

In our lives, the chakras themselves serve a fundamental role. Chakra, in a sense, serves as the link between our body and our spiritual energies. They also give us the ability to interact with our spiritual energy to encourage our overall well-being. However, to bridge this connection, you must first become conscious of your chakras and develop a deeper understanding of their work. Another thing that is sometimes lost is the value of maintaining a strong, positive bond with the inner self and providing an organized process to establish that bond so that the rational brain knows how to preserve that relationship.

By beginning to understand chakras, you can start to comprehend how your sphere of energy functions, and what you can do to connect meaningfully and impactful with your field of energy. Through such an exercise, you will also find yourself in nearly every possible manner creating a more profound sense of tranquility and balance within yourself and your life.

1

UNDERSTANDING YOUR ENERGY: THE EN-ERGY AND HOW IT AFFECTS US

"Do the thing you have been afraid to do."

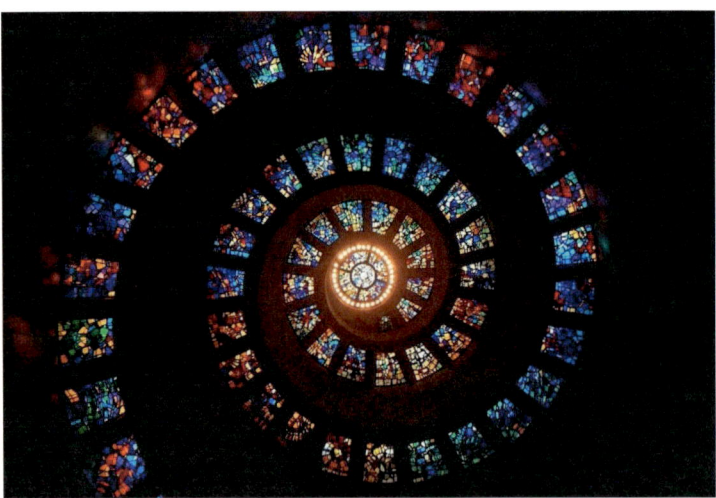

In this chapter, I will unpack the forms of energy based on their sources and how they are channeled from person to person. I will also talk about how we receive energy, and the effects it has on us; in other words, our responses.

Energy forms

Human energy takes forms in the things we can feel, and that is why they are more impactful because feelings can last a lifetime. Our senses are the major pathways for channeling energy from our surroundings into our bodies. The things our eyes see, what we hear, smell, etc. tell us something about our current situation all the time; it could be a pleasant situation, an alarming one, or a painful one. The energy we receive presents itself in the form of information. The information we obtain about things we experience or situations in which we find ourselves prompts us to take action, thereby influencing us. Still, the response we give is dependent on our personal or inherent energy. Based on the source or mostly who it is coming from, and its intent, the form of energy could be positive, neutral, or adverse. Let us look at this example if you hear on the news that a big company or organization, like Shell or McDonalds, is folding due to bankruptcy. It is a hypothetical fact. The news agency or reporter's motive is to inform people by giving them news updates making the intention neutral from the source because they are not telling the masses which action to take. To the competitors, this will be good news, to the stock trader, a call to action, but to the investors and staff of these companies, definitely bad news. However, each member of these groups' efforts in response to the news is dependent on their energies.

Influence

When the effect of an emitted energy prompts you to take action in favor of its source, we call it an influence, and it may be good or bad. Great leaders and historical icons have been able to persuade masses to assist them in realizing their visions. They could only achieve such because, though the vision or dream may have initially been one man's, they could connect with people who had similar goals, thereby influencing them. A fact is that we affect other people either directly or indirectly, and it could be from factors like our actions to vague reasons such as simply existing. Yes, someone's life can change because you exist. For example, a friend of mine changed his bad sleeping habit because he always saw an older man reading books on his balcony very early in the morning. My friend usually stayed up late doing unproductive things he called them), and the next day, my colleague would have problems at work, or he would be com (as he called them), and the next day, my friend would have problems at work, or he would be complaining that he wasted that day, that he couldn't fulfill any personal goal. But every morning, while he was rushing, trying to prepare for work, he will see the man in his chair, calm like he had no problems or worries and the older man also went to work, so how could he manage to achieve such mornings that he had enough time to read before going to work? Without them, even meeting, that man's morning routine had influenced someone to fix his sleep life. There are so many other instances of direct and indirect influences people have had on other people, but what does it is the vibe those influencers were emitting at the people that look up to them.

Vessels

Apart from their primary function of serving as containers or jars, vessels often reshape whatever is put inside them, but that is only when they control what is put inside them. For example, if you pour water in a jar, as far as the jar can withstand the pressure of the water, the water takes the shape of the jar, but if you try to put bricks in the jar, then it becomes whether the bricks can fit in or not, but it does not change the shape of the brick. Not that it is not possible, but typically jars are not made for bricks, and neither are people with the different types of energy. Not all vibes will be compatible with you, but they will all come at you so, what do you do with this surge of energy?

Processing and response: Thoughts and outcomes

Having concluded that we respond to energies we receive from our environment, that is, vibe reception to response, we also have to look at what happens between these two stages. If you can gain control of this intermediate phase, you can always determine the response. The middle step is the thought process phase, and this is where you do all the decryption of the information your senses have collected.

2

CONTROLLING YOUR ENERGY I: MASTER-ING YOUR CHAKRA

"Calm but alert. Relaxed but ready. Smooth but sharp. Humble but confident.

Chakra

The Vedas defined the chakras as energy centers representing different aspects of your self, your life, your body, your emotions, your thoughts, and your spirit. The seven chakras located directly within your body, specifically, are ones that you can quickly work within your personal life. In comparison, you indirectly work with the 107 chakras in your afterlife or when you attain a higher level of spirituality. In general, these are not typically chakras you will work with on your own. However, you may desire to set the intention to have them balanced and harmonized during specific meditation experiences.

Prana

The Vedas defines the Prana as life force energy that exists within each chakra. It also says that Prana is responsible for creating the entire experience of chakras, ranging from physical, mental, emotional, and spiritual experiences. Individuals can affect the Prana of their chakras through practical means such as through diet, meditation, reiki, and yoga. Other ways to affect chakra are through color therapy, crystals, and other forms of energy work that allow you to bring peace and harmony to your chakras. However, the primary methods used in affecting Prana were meditation, yoga, and diet.

Description of chakras

People commonly believed that the chakras are flat discs of energy that spin in a clockwise manner over a central axis point located on your chakra pillar, or within the spiritual body. The seven chakras we work with regularly are located on a pillar that is arranged down the spine, and they all have their individual "central axis" around which they can spin. However, there are some different dogmas on where these axes exist and what the chakras look like. There is a belief that each chakra has one axis located within, below, or above the spine and rotates about it, while others believe that there are two axes points. There is one in front of the spine, and one behind it such that each axes point has two discs mirroring each other and spinning in a clockwise motion along the spine. When there is chakra imbalance, the chakra may leave its original axis point and begin to turn too fast, too slow, or even in the opposite direction. To balance the chakra, one would have to work with the Prana bring it back into a Gentle, consistent rotation on its primary axis.

Apart from being assigned specific locations, shapes, and directions, chakras have distinct distinctive colours, symbols, and names. The seven chakras located within the body are red, orange, yellow, green, blue, indigo, and violet, similar to the rainbow colours. Also, each disc glows in their specific colours boldly and vibrantly way when they are balanced. A chakra imbalance could also lead to a very bright or dim glow that you can barely see the colour at all.

What Chakras do

Chakras serve a deep purpose in our lives by bridging the connection between our body and our spiritual energy, thereby linking us with our spiritual energy in a way that supports our overall wellbeing. To be able to bridge this connection, however, you must first become aware of your chakras and develop a deeper understanding of what they are and how they work.

An essential tool forgotten in modern society is the importance of having a deep, meaningful connection with your spiritual self and having an organized method for creating that connection so that your logical brain understands how to nurture it. With chakras, you gain a unique and thorough perspective on how your energy fields work and how you can work with them to create optimal health. The way you gain access to this optimal health is through what is commonly known as "holistic." It means recognizing your entire self as a whole, intimately interconnected beings, and achieving optimal health. This includes your physical, mental, emotional, and spiritual wellbeing.

The integration of chakras concepts and being able to work with them to create optimal health in your spirit, you will, in turn, create optimal health within the rest of your body. By understanding this, you realize that to achieve optimal health, you have to treat specific ailments by working on individual chakras. However, it would help if you also worked with all of your chakras to ensure that they stay balanced.

Vibes

The chakras are responsible for leading spiritual energy. They do so by interacting with the energy within the body, and outside of your body, called an aura. The aura represents the non-physical energy that exists around a person all the time. Most people describe aura as a large egg-shaped dome of energy that surrounds each of us, and that we manipulate it with our minds and emotions. You can experience someone's aura by merely being around someone experiencing a strong thought or emotion, even if they are not outwardly expressing it. Most people explain this experience as intuition or a "vibe."

Chakra's effect on physical experience

In matters of well-being, anything you experience in your energy field will manifest into your emotional, mental, and then physical area if not fixed in your energy (spiritual) field. So, if you lack awareness of your spiritual self, there is a possibility you are entirely missing out on the root cause of whatever experience you are having hence the unnecessary challenges we face while dealing with some issues. Linking this to how energies from the environment influence yours, we can say that your energy is like a public computer, which different people use frequently. Without a sound chakra management system, like an anti-virus, then the computer will often have issues.

The chakras

The root chakra

The root chakra, known as Muladhara in Sanskrit, is located at the base of your tailbone. Sometimes, the root chakra is also called the base chakra, or the first chakra. This chakra's primary function is to support your primordial brain, which is the part of your brain responsible for survival. All of your survival instincts and primal urges are in this energy field, and the root chakra controls them. The color red represents the root chakra. As you grow, the root chakra aids in you, forming a sense of identity and belonging within your family and your community. From an intuitive level, you know that you need to be connected with your community to survive, as survival truly comes from strength in numbers. The root chakra will thrive and have a strong foundation when there are feelings of safety, support, and provision. However, growing up without these feelings causes root chakra imbalance, and most times, the people may act out in ways that further feeds into that imbalance. The root chakra is also associated with the desire to eat, copulate, seek or maintain shelter, or otherwise survive. Also, when you find yourself working towards loyalty to your family, friends, and feelings of caring, nurturing, or protection of your family, friends, or community, you are experiencing the energy of your root chakra.

There are particular messages associated with each chakra. The root chakra philosophy is primarily about the importance of understanding your power and using it to break away from emotional bondage while still taking your well-being into your own hands. Instead of depending on someone to care for and defend you, be prepared to do so yourself. Experience the sense of strength and confidence that comes with knowing that you can do this on your own. When you continue to understand the value of this teaching and incorporate it into your own life, you find that your connections with the people around you are starting to flourish.

The sacral chakra

The sacral chakra, known as Svadhisthana, is located about three finger-widths below your navel. This chakra, also referred to as your second chakra, controls your need for close relationships and your ability to regulate the complexities of your physical environment. Although this chakra relates to the bond and the community, it reflects more intensely on the unique relationships between you and each person in your life, including yourself. You must maintain harmony in your root chakra to work in your sacral chakra. The balance in your root chakra will encourage you to feel closeness within your community. In contrast, the balance in your sacral chakra will intensify that affection and get even more out of that connection. The sacral chakra is depicted in the color orange.

Your sacral chakra is home to your sexuality, creativity, and intimacy. Any emotion you experience from fulfilling your passions to strengthening your friendship and developing stronger feelings of connection with others around you is always connected with your sacral chakra. Your sacral chakra tries to encourage you to build your means of self-expression in whatever way you can, using the senses and sensory awareness to do so. Your sacral chakra's energies generate your individuality, your positions in life, and your sense of personal identity.

The sacral chakra aims to show you the value of knowing your potential and taking care of your destiny. If you have a healthy, balanced sacral chakra, it becomes effortless for you to realize who you are, engage with others, enjoy interpersonal relationships, and share healthy relational interaction with the people around you. There is no co-dependency, outward quest for affirmation, or the need for immediate satisfaction of excitement and desire. Inside you, you know that you can build all of that yourself. It's important to understand that any relationship you have in your life, from friends to family or intimate relationships, has a reason.

The solar plexus chakra

The solar plexus chakra is also known as Manipura is the third of your seven body chakras, and is often referred to as the "seat of your soul." It is still considered to be one of the lower chakras. But this is where your soul continues to bind to the physical life. Here, you are starting to move high enough towards the energetic foundation that you are pulling out of your purely natural impulses and powers and are beginning to achieve higher levels of consciousness and knowledge. The solar plexus chakra is the center of your character and ego, and its representative color is yellow. The energy here is connected to the sun, and it relates to the blazing energy that you may feel in this particular area of your body, as well as your energy core. Working with your solar plexus chakra sounds like you reaching into the most critical aspects of yourself because you can find yourself feeling a magnetic bond to the root of who you are. When you are fully balanced and healthy, you will be motivated, in a modest way, by vast amounts of self-confidence and self-esteem.

The solar plexus chakra shows you how important it is to love and like yourself. By establishing a positive connection for yourself, you find yourself motivated to step beyond all that gets by your way of life. If you cannot build a positive interaction with yourself, you will find yourself making choices that may be detrimental to yourself or damage to that for which you care. It can be very tempting to act in a self-sabotaging way if you don't have enough respect and consideration for yourself. If you genuinely work within the solar plexus chakra lessons, you will know how to love yourself and make decisions from a position where you love yourself, and that enables you to value yourself more. You will understand that self-love is not vain or selfish, but one of the most caring things you can do for yourself.

The heart chakra

The heart chakra, known as Anahata in Sanskrit, is located right where the heart is in the middle of your chest. The color green portrays this chakra, but many times pink is associated with it, just as pink appears to be a very soft, nurturing, and emotional color for others. The heart chakra controls your feelings, your genuine affection, and your capacity to recover at an emotional level. Your heart chakra is full of thousands of emotional memories that you have experienced throughout your life. It will remain open to the creation of new emotional memories as long as you live.

The heart chakra is the core of all feelings, so it's a very delicate, fragile, and often painful chakra with which to deal. When you work on your heart chakra, you are likely to experience everything from feelings of pain and sadness to true love and self-acceptance. Feeling the full spectrum of your emotions is normal and familiar with your heart chakra, and that should be acknowledged whenever you consciously work with your heart chakra. Heart chakra activity may end up crying, smiling, furious, quickening your heartbeat, feeling calm, or feeling other emotions in your broad spectrum of human emotions. Accepting this and embracing yourself unquestioningly through it is essential to connect consciously through your heart chakra while enabling yourself to feel healing and peace. As you work with your heart chakra, you can improve the strength of your practice by learning how to consciously and intuitively manipulate your feelings in a manner that reflects the highest good and the highest good of all. By the end of the day, your heart chakra wants to see, feel, and show true love to everybody, even though that's not how you are currently feeling.

While the solar plexus chakra communicates through ego, the heart chakra communicates through your higher self and continually encourages you to expand into a more significant state of love. Your heart chakra wants you to surrender as deeply to love as possible in every area of your life. The more you can do so, the more you will be living in your purest possible form.

The throat chakra

The throat chakra, called Vishuddha in Sanskrit, is found at the base of your throat, right in the baseline where your neck meets your arms. The chakra is defined by the color blue and is activated by the force of thought, language, and interactions that you share with yourself and others. The throat chakra may affect several dimensions, ranging from inside yourself to between yourself and others, and in broader ways, such as by global effects. Considering how healthy the throat chakra is, it can also have severe and long-lasting implications. Knowing how to manage and function through your throat chakra is vital if you're going to have a strong, substantive effect on your throat chakra. As mammals, our throat chakras can bind, defend, or divide us, making them necessary for survival.

Throat chakra serves as a path for energy passage from your lower chakras to your head, and from your head to your lower chakras. The throat chakra functions to listen to and collect knowledge about the outer world, or the inner life, and transfer it to the lower body. For example, if you hear music that you consider encouraging or uplifting, it could bring a feeling of calm and relaxation to your whole body. However, should you encounter something that you find disturbing or disquieting, it will give you feelings of fear and anticipation in your body. The same goes for everything you say either out loud or to yourself in your head, and you must do your best to say things about yourself and others from the point of goodness and honesty. The throat chakra teaches you the importance of speaking up, offering forgiveness, connecting kindly, and asserting your truth. It would help if you always allowed yourself to speak up when you need to, as not doing so can result in you being trapped in unwanted situations that could be damaging for your wellbeing. Anytime you repress what you want to say because you believe you are not allowed to or entitled to share your thoughts or opinions, you find yourself in a position where you deny the power of your throat chakra. Rather than doing so, you should always kindly speak up and assert yourself. You never know what opportunities could come from expressing your wants and needs.

The third eye chakra

The third eye chakra, also referred to as the forehead chakra, is called Ajna in Sanskrit. This chakra reflects your intellectual capacity, emotions, and the ability to determine your values and attitudes. It's also the core where you'll experience extrasensory skills if you choose to hone yours and function properly. The color of the indigo depicts the third eye chakra, and many people see it as being in the shape of a third eye in the middle of your forehead, allowing you a "vision" of things beyond the physical.

Your third eye chakra is a highly intuitive energy core that helps you perceive and interact with otherworldly powers, like those that reside right here between us and those that are far apart. Any knowledge that you already have, or that you appear to "just acquire" along the way, will be absorbed via your third eye chakra. This wisdom can be both positive and negative. It can be derived from any form of energy ranging from physical humans to information that you can channel or obtain from higher energy sources.

The third eye teachings say that your life path is not determined by any one person or any group of people. Your life path is defined by your unique life experiences and what you desire and believe to be true in your life. You have to be mindful of the coercion or pressure from the outside world to change the reality or to operate in line with someone else's fact rather than the own. And if you're especially close to a person or a community of people, it's healthy, common, and reasonable to disagree about specific issues and follow your life direction against the person or group's beliefs. You don't have to fall under someone else's reality, except your own, and it's rational for you to choose to live your life your way.

The crown chakra

The crown chakra is one of the purest, most straightforward, and reliable forces that you can encounter throughout your human lifetime. In reality, this chakra has very few correspondences, modes of energy, perceptions, and teachings, although they are incredibly insightful and vital. Allowing yourself to work with your crown chakra would significantly strengthen your relationship with divine forces, which will also complete your practice with your seven primary chakras. The crown chakra is also called Sahasrara in Sanskrit, is the seventh and final chakra on your physical body. This chakra is located at the crown of your head, just above your physical body, and it is represented by the color violet, though some people see this energy as being white due to how pure and clean it is. The crown chakra governs your connection to pure divine energy. It allows you to effortlessly draw forth a sense of connection and support from the universe, or whichever higher power energy in which you choose to believe and have faith.

The crown chakra's primary function is to be a portal or an entry point into the physical body, where life force energy will circulate freely across the whole system. When you have an open crown chakra, the greater universe's energy can shower abundantly through you, activate all the energies and powers of the universe within your very body, and thereby further empower and balance your lower chakras. The crown chakra wants to teach you how to exist within your humanity without being completely alone. It wants you to understand that you are disconnected from others around you because you are an entity, but that you have a stronger sense of interaction with every person around you than you are likely to think. You are close to those around you, and each one of you has the same relation to the same fundamental force.

How to maintain you chakra

Knowing how essential chakra is to human energy, and that there is a time when we experience chakra imbalance, it is pertinent that we take care of them. Below are some methods you can adopt to maintain your chakra.

Eat a chakra-replenishing or boosting diet

In the anime world, of ninjas and martial artists, there are many references to chakra and chakra enhancing diets like the "chakra pill." For theatrics, they are usually drug-like pellets the characters can take at any time, like during combat. Still, in reality, chakra enhancing meals require an essential ingredient of being colorful. If you recall, all the chakras have colors, so a very unusual diet helps kick-start your chakra for the day. Eating as many different brightly colored fresh fruits and vegetables as possible will ensure that you incorporate the energy of each of your chakras directly into your body in a practical, physical way. This is not only great for your chakras but also great for your body in general. In a manner, this will strengthen your physical immune system and your spiritual immunity system, so that you are more resilient to the physical and energy domains.

Yoga and meditation

Yoga was initially designed as a practice that was meant to help facilitate meditation though many people now use it for exercise. Its original purpose was to clear and cleanse your physical body from specific energies so that you could engage with the spiritual realm and the energy of meditation. If you wish to have an excellent, intense meditation session, learn how to use yoga properly to cleanse the physical body so that you are prepared for a passionate, efficient meditation session. Preferably, you should meditate during yoga, and then you should switch effortlessly from a yoga session to a quiet meditation activity.

Self-Awareness and Mindfulness

In our urban society, self-awareness is not something we seem to do well with. Instead of acknowledging ourselves, our talents, and our perspectives, we are encouraged to change them so that we can do what other people need us to do instead. We need to rediscover what our needs are and pay close attention to the different cues that indicate that those needs are ready to be met. You may be shocked to find that, as you improve your self-awareness and mindfulness, you tend to note your desires and how you act much earlier than you have ever noticed before. This early recognition of your emotions, desires, and even energy levels helps you start fighting for yourself and do what you need to do to keep your energy balanced. When you achieve this level of self-care, controlling the chakras is much more natural as you can do that much more for yourself. The benefits will be felt in your energy, mind, emotions, and body. Ultimately, you will begin to thrive far more in your entire life if you find yourself experiencing a more positive capacity to engage in self-awareness and mindfulness in your day to day life.

3

CONTROLLING YOUR ENERGY II: MINDFULNESS

"The mind is like water. When it is turbulent, everything is difficult to see. When it is calm, everything becomes clear."

Mindfulness involves cultivating a moment-by-moment perception of our emotions, desires, body experiences, and natural atmosphere through a soft, caring focus. Mindfulness also requires tolerance, which means that we pay attention to our emotions and feelings without criticizing them or assuming, for example, that there is a right or wrong way to think or act at a precise moment. Throughout life, both within our minds and in our cultures, we have the ideal circumstances to indulge in. In other words, everything we do seems to be incredibly repetitive and routine, and our brain loves it. Our brains use this routine and regular experience to create a multitude of habit loops that enable our conscious mind to gain full control so that we can live our lives through our subconscious mind's automation. Our day-to-day interactions are as natural as breathing or pumping blood from our hearts and into our bodies. Often, people who engage in severe level automation in their lives end up using their extra mental energy to self-sabotage, worry, create stress, or more disorder. Furthermore, they tend to generate hardship or exacerbate anxiety and stress can become habitual, leaving you feeling as though you are in a chronic state of automation and stress. Unless you learn to break the habit, it only gets worse and worse.

The practice of mindfulness has an incredibly powerful ability to teach you how to develop your self-awareness. As you begin to develop your mindfulness practice, you will find yourself experiencing a more profound sense of understanding about yourself, the world around you, and how you interact with the world around you. The practice of mindfulness has an incredibly powerful ability to teach you how to develop your self-awareness. As you begin to develop your mindfulness practice, you will find yourself experiencing a more profound sense of understanding about yourself, the world around you, and how you interact with the world around you.

Breathing in mindfulness

Breathing is the foundation of mindfulness because it is one of the most straightforward and most flexible practices that can help you connect with and focus on your body in the present situation. Like many aspects of life, we usually leave our breathing to our automated processes instead of focusing on other things, such as stress, worry, or frustration. While many practices can divert your attention away from these feelings, few are as versatile, simple, and mobile as your breathing. Simply put, your breath is with you everywhere you go, and whether you are focusing on it or not, it is happening on its own at every moment of every day. When you experience a lack of mindfulness in your life, you can connect to your breath at any given moment for any time to experience a deepened level of connection with yourself, and a higher state of awareness. Thus, it is incredibly crucial that you invest energy in mindfulness breathing and practice it daily as often as possible.

Mindfulness breathing patterns

Square breath

Square breathing is a type of conscious breathing that allows you to indulge in equal parts by inhaling, retaining, exhaling, and holding back before inhaling. It would help if you used the square breath to stabilize your breathing better and control your nervous system and emotional functions, helping you to experience life from a more relaxed and peaceful viewpoint. The most common rhythm used for square breathing is a four-four-four-four rhythm. So, you're going to inhale the count of four, hold the count of four, exhale the count of four, and hold four before you start your next breath. You would usually need to repeat the breathing cycle 10-15 times to get the most value out of the breathing pattern. However, it would help if you indulged in a breathing routine for as little to as long as you feel relaxed with this mindfulness exercise.

The 5-7-8 breath

To indulge in a five-seven-eight breath, proceed by breathing through your nose to the count of five, then retain it to the count of seven, and exhale through your mouth to the count of eight. That breath will cause your head to feel light if you're not used to taking these heavy and long breaths, so you may want to sit down while doing it. As well, you're just expected to do it three to five times at first and work up to be able to do 10-15 in a row. You can follow the 3-5 breaths and then continue the normal breathing rhythm for a few more breaths until you take another 3-5 breaths before you have completed a total of 10-15. With this being said, do check in with your body and be aware of how you feel and make sure you're happy with the entire experience.

The Building-Decreasing Breath

Building-decreasing breathing is less about counting or breathing for some fixed time, and more about tracking where you're taking your breath. When we are nervous, anxious, afraid, exhausted, or some other stressful emotion, we frequently find ourselves engaging in quick, shallow breaths. Many times, people are agitated that they indulge in these breaths nearly entirely and never return to a regular deep breathing pattern, including when they are sleeping. Building-decreasing meditation will help you break the loop so that you can slowly lengthen and intensify your breath every single day before you breathe comfortably and peacefully through times of relaxation or mindfulness. To engage in building-decreasing breathing, you start by keeping your posture tall and your spine straight to quickly expand your stomach and chest area. When you're ready, you'll inhale through your nose, fill your belly and diaphragm first, fill your lungs, and then fill your throat. You'll expel the breath from your mouth, lungs, and then your diaphragm and stomach. As you inhale, your stomach and lungs should expand, and when you exhale your chest, your stomach will sink to your body.

4

CONTROLLING YOUR ENERGY III: AWARENESS OF THE PRESENT

"The happiest people spend most of their time evaluating and improving themselves. The unhappiest people spend most of their day and time criticizing and evaluating others."

One of the easiest ways of getting lost in our emotions, memories, or the information we receive about our current situation is when we lose our awareness. Many are so caught up in the past or anxious about the future that they forget that it is the present that needs their immediate attention. Learning to be aware of the gift is a crucial tool in manipulating your energy in your favor, thereby changing your life for the better. Awareness itself can be seen as a journey of mindfulness. Via awareness, you can recognize the need for mindfulness, build knowledge, and decide how your mindfulness can increase your journey's consistency. Indeed, there is no mindful path without awareness, and there is no awareness without mindfulness. These two states go side-by-side to assist you in experiencing the best possible journey.

The essence of the present

Honoring the present time does not mean you are no longer able to talk about the past or the future. On the contrary, occasionally relaxing with your memories is a great way to reconnect with the things you love or resolve the problems you're dealing with. Likewise, spending some time contemplating the future allows you to decide what you want for yourself and towards what you're working. When you know what you want and what you're working for, you can work towards it with a great deal of consistency, concentration, and commitment.

In the present, you will have access to everything you could need. Here, you gain liberation from the torment of your past or the things you wish you could change. With the present, you can incorporate the improvements you want to you had made before, and you can do some great things to obtain the relationship you know you're missing from the past. You will also achieve independence from the uncertainties of the future by releasing control of the future and believing that it will happen as it will. In doing so, you will take some of the burdens off yourself and start enjoying life for what it is, rather than having to play lord of the universe over every aspect of your life.

Releasing the future and the past

Do you want to improve your future? Set some goals and draft plans for achieving those goals. When goals aren't set, and plans aren't made, it could lead to unhealthy doses of anxiety, and sometimes it leads to depression. Sometimes, procrastination sets in because you keep spending time; you would have used to take action thinking about what the outcome of the future will be. As far as your perception is concerned, the past can be a rather tricky and clinging subject. The past can hold on to you.

Through the power of negative or positive emotions, although each scenario would be for a variety of reasons. If you feel negative emotions about your past, you are likely stuck with unresolved issues that make you feel hurt, angry, or upset in your present situation. If you have positive emotions about your memories to the extent that you're stuck on them, you're apt to cling on to your memory because it seems better than your current situation. In either scenario, the past doesn't help you enjoy your life, but instead, it's holding you back and making it more difficult for you to embrace what life has to offer you right now. The best way to address the past is to accept that what has happened has already happened and that you can only use it to teach you or to help you find a way to improve your present moment. If you hold on to depressive emotions, it might be time to forgive a particular person or circumstance or seek therapy and develop healthy coping strategies. If you harbor positive feelings, it may be time for you to learn how those positive emotions were created so that you can create more of them in your present moment. Either way, the past exists to teach you how to improve your present and your future. The sooner you learn those lessons, the sooner you will be able to stop living in your past and begin to make it a useful and peaceful accessory to your life.

Staying in the present

One of the simplest and most effective ways to stay in the present is to shift your mindset to the present moment anytime you find yourself wrapped up in the past or the future. Begin by recognizing why you have lived in the past or the future in the first place. There's something there that you're stuck on and that you need to accept before you can formally remove that particular thought or concern. When you know what it is, you can either make a plan to recover or remove it or make a plan to execute it time so you can stop thinking about it in the present.

5

CONTROLLING YOUR ENERGY IV: MORE ON THE PAST, THE PRESENT AND THE FUTURE

The present moment is all that we have in life at any given time, and it is our responsibility to make the most of it. Many of us are so caught living in the past or living in the future that we cannot live in today. It does make sense, too. The past is embedded in our subconscious through our memories and feelings. When you encounter or feel something that activates a memory, it is not unusual to have those memories triggered. The future is included in our calendar and tells us regularly what we need to do in the future, whether you are going to the hair salon or buy your first house before you are 30 years old. It also makes sense that so many people fail to slow down and live in the present moment, given how much focus we put on our history and future. However, when we think about the moment, we lose out on what we've got. We lose out on everything that we have. Remember, you can't go back and relive those memories or change them, and you can't go forward and manipulate the future, so it turns out exactly as you expected. Only taking care of the present moment is all you can do.

Letting go of the past

The past houses all your memories, joys, happiness, achievements, regrets, etc. Releasing the past is partly about your mentality, partly about recovery, and partly about breaking up patterns that could hold you stuck to thinking about the past. If you can concentrate on changing these three areas of your life, you can start suppressing the past's influence to enhance the ability to stay present in the moment. Freeing yourself from the past can be aided by mindset, but sometimes it takes a lot more than a shift in perspective to help you truly heal. Although it can be helpful to recognize that you need to use the past as a tool to learn better for the present and future, it can be challenging to leave it. If you feel a significant amount of painful or overwhelming emotions about the past, it can be helpful to step into some serious healing so that you can let it go. Counseling or therapy is a great way to engage in healing from your past. You can also use journaling, talking, prayer, and surrounding yourself with supportive and loving individuals to help you move through a phase of healing. Also, be sure to allow yourself to express and release your emotions so that you can let go of them and move on for good.

You will have a fresh perspective on the past at some point in time. You will feel as if the problems are being resolved. You will be able to achieve a sense of closure and trigger the healing cycle to accept the new mentality formally and fully. You'll need to objectively determine at this stage what your patterns surround the past. It's not unusual for people to be trapped out of habit in the past for a while. Understand that this can be just as harmful as being stuck out of guilt or a lack of healing.

Letting go of the future

It's not unusual for people to find themselves worried about the future and habitually stay in that role. So if you want to loosen the grip that the future holds over you, you'll need to change your perception about the future, embrace optimism, and learn how to trust your action plan. Your mindset around the future should ideally focus on detachment and helping you remain more open to what could happen in your future. From a young age, we are taught that our plans for our future, and our ability to fulfill those plans, mean a great deal about who we are and how worthy we are. Right from a young age, we watch people who choose to stick with the same sports or activities throughout the school are put on a pedestal while everyone else is "average." This continues throughout adulthood as our friends choose colleges and may get good-paying jobs, start families, get promotions, and otherwise advance with "the plan." Someone who can make a plan and stick to it is considered a miraculous person of sorts, while those who struggle to find out or see things through are shamed for not being clear, focused, or serious about their lives.

This whole scenario will make it very possible for you to become intensely attached to your future and therefore be nervous and anxious about how it will turn out. As an adult, you will be concerned about everything from whether you live up to the standards of others, whether or not you will be able to pay bills this month, or whether you will be able to satisfy all of your responsibilities. All this can be released if you want to remove yourself from the future and trust in the process. What you should do is to create a plan for yourself, and then concentrate more on implementing the plan for now, and less about thinking about whether or not the plan is good enough or even efficient to achieve the results you want. By maintaining your fear or anxiety, the future can be used to help the development without being a tool against you.

In addition to independence, acknowledging the unpredictable nature of the future serves to help you build a positive view of the future. Through acknowledgment, you provide yourself with the requisite degree of stability to comfortably handle whatever can happen in the future. That way, when things don't go as planned, you can remain comfortable, and you can embrace them for what they are and keep going forward regardless. The freedom you achieve by embracing guarantees that you can distance yourself much more from the future. And when doing so, that you can fully appreciate the present moment. Trust is another thing that you must focus on improving in your life when it comes to letting go of the future. It is going to make sense to sit down and draw up a plan for how you anticipate you will experience the future at various points in your life. For example, at the beginning of the week, you can write down your weekly obligations, at the beginning of the month you can write down your monthly obligations, and at the beginning of the year, you can write out your yearly goals and plans. You may also make a long term plan for yourself based on your personal goals and what you hope to experience in your future. The key is to make a plan that you can trust in, and then to believe in the plan and follow it as you have created it. The more you can trust in your plan, the easier it will be for you to fully detach from the future and accept whatever comes up as it comes up.

The present and how to stay in it

The present for you is here, and now, it is your control room, and you are the controller. It is in the present that you can determine the future and learn from the past. You must put more effort into staying in the present and make the most out of it, because it will be the new past, and the future will be the new present. The best way to begin integrating yourself in the present moment is by redirecting your awareness to the present moment anytime you find yourself caught up in the past or future. To effectively do so, start by identifying why you were dwelling on the past or future in the first place. There is a piece of information there that you are lingering on and that you need to embrace before you can officially release that particular memory or worry. Once you know what it is, you can either make a plan to heal or release it or make a plan to plan it out or prepare for it during a specific time so that you can stop worrying about it in the meantime. Make sure you write down whatever you have resolved to do to heal or release something or take the first steps of a plan for resolution so that you can officially move past it.

You will start to incorporate your mind in the present moment when you begin to release the desire for a connection to a past memory or a future concern. Start by breathing and getting connected to your body. Finally, in the present moment, spend several moments calming yourself by realizing what your five senses are feeling. Think about what you're doing, doing, feeling, smelling, and degusting right now, and how it makes you feel and what thoughts it gives you. Then, think of what you should do right now to help you get the most out of this moment and do it. Practice and concentrate all of your time and attention on that thing to be as present as long as possible.

6

AMPLIFYING YOUR ENERGY I: FIND YOUR FLUX

"Pay attention to who your energy increases and decreases around because that is the universe giving you a hint of who you should embrace or stray from."

BFFs and lovers

In a survey, the people were asked to answer these questions; how did you find your true love? How did you find your dream career, and how did you end up with your best friends? We hear things like a dream career, best career, lovers, and the acronym, BFF almost everywhere. By the way, BFF stands for "Best Friends Forever." After assessing many answers, one key factor was prominent in all the answers, and it was compatible. Not because of a better offer, not because we grew up in the same neighborhood, and certainly not because it was love at first sight. All the genuine answers pointed out that the participants were in those positions because they found what most people looked for endlessly, and that is pure satisfaction. You derive real pleasure when you find compatibility because your energy easily synchronizes with the energy in the environment and gets amplified. You will hardly find conflicts of interest in such situations because they usually pursue similar goals and live by the same principles.

The other reason is that you become more potent when the number increases. People often debate on the appropriateness of this statement, "If you can't beat them, join them." People argue whether it is ideal for joining the majority of opposing them and becoming the minority. What amplifying your energy teaches is that joining the majority can be for the better if the group in question has positive values because, in reality, the majority isn't always the villain.

"You deserve people in life who understand that you are too good and too important to lose."

Ways of detecting your compatibility with a person or a situation

- **Sharing common interest:** common interest is what positivity feeds on. To share a common interest with someone means that you and somebody else have the same interest. Imagine that the word "interest" is a piece of cloth. You have it in your hand. Another person then holds that same "interest" in his hand.

- **Collective improvement:** sharing similar interests or views goes a long way in identifying compatibility. When the other person or situation shows you that your desires are integrated into shared interest or set goals, there will be compatibility.

- **Intuition:** when a person says, "I like your vibe," or "I've got a good hunch about you," that is the person's energy binding with the other person's energy, and subsequently, an influence follows.

The issue with amplifying your energy is that you must first correct yourself, ensuring that you have only positive vibes because, if your energy is negative, your "good hunch" can be and will be towards negative energy too. Unlocking your positivity creates the ability for you to understand or know something without any direct evidence or reasoning process.

People may not tell you how they feel about you, but they always show you. Pay attention. Trust your instincts. Intuition doesn't lie. Never apologize for trusting your intuition – your brain can play tricks, your heart can blind you sometimes, but your gut is always right. There is a voice that doesn't use words. Listen. So many of us loved with a love that was more than love. However, the most potent energy that can be unlocked is loving oneself at the beginning of a lifelong romance. Love is the energy of life.

7

AMPLIFYING YOUR ENERGY II: LOVE AND OTHER EMOTIONAL ENERGIES

It would be inappropriate to talk about energy without talking about love because love is one of the highest forms of energy in the universe. Not only is love a form of energy, but it also serves as a necessity. In terms of emotional feelings, love is not the only source or form of energy, hatred is also there, and you can't talk about love without addressing its opposite. There is a constant need to address negative emotions because, in most cases, when love has been abused and becomes corrupted, people (especially the victims) easily fall for the next available emotional energy. Unfortunately, the emotional energies the victims easily sync with at that point are usually those of negative vibes, with hatred at the top of the chart. As humans, in an ideal scenario, love is the first energy we feel from birth. Feelings and emotions are only the creation of mind and energy. Love always brings difficulties, that is true, but the right side of it is that it gives energy. Love is infectious and the greatest healing energy. Love is the creation of the soul.

Relationships

One of the ways love energy, or emotional energy, in general, is transferred from person to person is via relationships. Knowing that humans are social beings, it is only natural for humans to crave a sense of belonging, which is achieved by being in a relationship. So how exactly can a relationship be defined? A relationship is defined as a connection between two individuals. It is a bond of intimacy that two or more people feel towards each other. This concept is rather broad and varies from person to person. Each individual has a unique way of defining his or her relationship, but, overall, it indicates a state of interconnection, especially an emotional connection. Every relationship in our life is interlinked and grows into a finely connected network. When we sustain strong, healthy relationships in our lives, we accomplish peace of mind. Successful relationships give our lives meaning, grace, and joy, and that is why it is essential to be able to change this aspect of your life whenever you notice misappropriation. The issue here is that such changes cannot be easily made if you do not have control of this aspect of your life, and to have control, and you need to know the type of connections you have in these relationships.

There are different types of relationships, and knowing the kind of a relationship you are in and the terms of the relationship goes a long determining the types of vibes that are distributed through such connections.

Family

A family, when described, narrowly entails two or more people who are related to each other by birth, adoption, or marriage and live in the same house. These people are an individual's first interaction and are mostly a source of attachment. The majority of the time, these relationships offer support, mutual trust, shared values and beliefs, and a strong sense of belonging. However, in the past three decades, the concept of family has evolved. Even non-traditional family structures now offer comfort and support.

Platonic Relationship

A platonic relationship is also referred to as friendship, and It is a close tie among two individuals that are often built upon common experiences, shared interests, nearness, and emotional bonding. A platonic relation specifically is a connection between two individuals without any sexual desires. The thin relationship is mostly an informal one, where friends can turn to each other whenever they need each other. Today, social media has also led to such friendships; however, if you only communicate online, then it isn't considered as close friendships according to research. Over time, these platonic relationships may end in a romantic relationship, possibly when the feelings are mutual among both individuals.

Romantic Partnerships

Romantic partnerships, including marriage, are intimate relationships created between two individuals built upon love, conviction, intimacy, and romantic love. This form of relationship is typically experienced with only one person at a time.

Professional

A professional association is a constant interaction between two people who conform to a set of recognized boundaries that are deemed suitable according to the ethical standards. These relationships generally fall into categories such as employer-employee, client-professional, society-professional and professional-professional relationships.

The difference between Personal and Professional Relationships

Understanding the difference between personal and professional relationships is the foundation for building a strong and healthy one. Clarity of the roles facilitates you in knowing what to expect in terms of interaction and, in turn, prevents you from the pitfalls of confusing the two. In both professional and personal relationships, individuals must respect each other and try hard to be rational, liable, and polite. However, beyond that, the two kinds of relationships deviate. The most obvious differences can be found in areas like:

The purpose of the relationship

Relationships, people give importance to the quality of the connection. Intimacy is an object in itself. It incorporates associations with friends and family. Support is offered by being there for them, caring for each other and wanting the best for them. Remember that the best relationship is one in which your love for each other exceeds your need for each other. What we often need is a connection to someone that is real and lasting. When you seek understanding, lead with positivity, relationships have the potential to fill your cup abundantly.

Trust

In social connections, we build trust by interacting and getting to know one another and looking at how the other individual behaves over time. On the other hand, we tend to stay skeptical in some relationships. We restrict trust to a certain point and are always on the lookout for flaws of the other people. You will not even put in too much effort to get to know the person because you are often programmed to look for red flags.

Compassion

For a relationship to foster, it is imperative to have empathy. However, this concept is also applied differently in both types of relations. Love is not without its flaws. The stronger the love, the more it tests you. Compassion and empathy will make true love persist. It is important to understand that compassion is not a relationship between the healer and the wounded. It's a relationship between equals.

Competition

Here is where we have a significant difference. Some associations, the attitude is usually friendly, and the level of competition is to the minimum. On the contrary, some connections can be all about competitiveness and jealousy. You might even face dishonesty and sabotage. Being clear on the dynamics can help you remain strategic and carve your way to success.

Having known some of the relationships out there, and what is expected of the people in the relationship, it makes channeling of emotional energy less tasking. Also, since we are focusing on your personal life as the starting point, more emphases and scenarios will be made towards personal relationships because it is our relationships, we can efficiently utilize our love energy.

Building and nurturing your relationship (Love life)

Most people fall under two categories in this section; the first is being single. And the other is those who are in a relationship. The ability to control our love energy is usually a tasking situation, whether for people in relationships or single people who are not. It is also not ideal to jump into a relationship for the purpose of balancing your emotional energy. This could be the precursor of many toxic relationships, so my recommendation will be to take things easy, be cautious and assertive of what you stand to gain from the relationship, and be sincere about what you have to offer. However, what people receive and what they end up giving in the relationship isn't always what they planned because as relationships grow, some plans are bound to change. It takes a high level of tolerance to remain loyal to the end. Relationships take time to grow and become healthy. Building is vital. It is the things you do to strengthen your bond, and they can be in the form of sharing personal stories, experiences, life lessons, honesty, transparency, and respect. Nourishing a relationship is also about creating good memories. While doing all of these things, both partners become stronger as a couple. Your significant other is that person that you can count on when you can't count on anyone else.

An excellent description of a healthy relationship is when both people are equally respected, supported, and satisfied, and the relationship itself is thriving because of these. Love is the key in personal relationships, and the success of the relationship shows how well you can control your love energy, which in turn, shows how much and to which direction you are changing your life. Before we address how to nurture your relationship, especially your love life with your partner, we have to identify the things that can affect your love energy in your relationship.

Infidelity

If you recall, we said that energy is pure, but the vessel or channel re-shapes it and gives it motives or purposes. When there is infidelity, that is, one or either partner is cheating, pretending to be something they are not in the presence of their partners, but most times, it backfires because there is no balance in the love energy anymore. It does not fit in its new vessel. You must understand that feelings will change over time, and the feeling of love you have for someone does not necessarily have to last forever. The two of you must remain honest with each other during this time. It is a terrible feeling to tell someone that you are not sure how you feel at the moment. You may not want to do this, but when you push them away without giving them any explanation, they will feel terrible. You cannot expect them to take a hint, and one of the worst things to do is to cheat on them. Cheating doesn't just have to be physical. It can be emotional, too. When you begin to lose your partner's feelings and start developing feelings for someone else, you need to talk to your partner before acting. If your behavior changes, your partner may have already perceived it. Your partner might experience something similar. You're going to feel awful when you have this discussion, but you haven't done anything wrong. So, make sure you have a conversation with your partner before you step out of line. Honesty is always the best.

When reality sets in

When you see couples having fun, you may think that all relationships are about fun and romance, but that is not the case. Several couples find a method to deal with their shortcomings and keep it moving. So, when such fantasies propel people into having intimate relationships and the reality of having to add relationship demands to their life, it can be overwhelming. When you start dating for the first time, you'll have higher tolerance levels as everything looks glittery. Things sometimes change after a while. You'll feel that both of you are just riding along. Small issues and minor problems can irritate you now, and you may find it challenging to forgive misjudgments or little mistakes. You may also stop feeling guilty for doing the wrong things. When you no longer feel compassionate toward your partner, it is evident that you think differently now. Things will change in any relationship, and there will come a time when there is a plateau. If you are irritated by the small issues that arise between the two of you, it is probably time for you to review your relationship.

Coming across more attractive people

In truth, you will come across someone more attractive than your partner. It happens all the time. This, however, does not mean you do not love your partner. There is nothing wrong if you want to appreciate someone's looks, but if you think about how it will be when you are with them, then there is something wrong at home. As mentioned earlier, it is a terrible idea to act on any attraction or feeling you have toward a person who is not your partner. This is a huge no-no. This is something that anybody will agree on. Having said that, most people sabotage their relationships when they act on their feelings or take things a little too far. It gets worse when you start texting and calling. If you continuously think about ending your relationship, you need to be conscious and make the right decision. It would be best if you either talked to your partner or shut these things down. If you feel very strongly about getting out of a relationship, they may feel very strongly about it too. Make sure you speak to your partner before you act in any situation like this. The conversation is going to be painful, but it is better than having to confess about doing something wrong. Also, while at it, if your partner notices a shift in behavior, you need to explain to them why you feel that way. You owe at least this much to them. You cannot leave them worrying about whether you will stay. This will only ruin their self-confidence. You will be the one to blame because you could never be honest. You should always think about how it would be if you were on the other end.

Distance and lack of communication

A lot of couples fall out of love due to a lack of healthy communication. When there is inadequate communication between partners, it is difficult to resolve conflicts that would have seemed insignificant if they had quality time. These couples no longer affirm their love and appreciation for one another. Couples who have been together for a long time sometimes begin to fail to communicate their feeling to their partners. These couples often refuse to discuss serious relationship issues. That's how the frustrations are piled up. So if negativity adds up, resentment will cause the relationship to become tense and unpleasant. Communication is a powerful component of a good relationship, and a lack of adequate interaction between partners could indeed disintegrate a relationship. Relationship distance is not being able to establish physical contact for different reasons. Intimacy is essential in love life, and so, when partners are distant, that piece is missing. Sometimes when the distance is inevitable and becomes stretched over a long period, it leaves negative impacts on the feelings people have for each other. It usually starts with fewer calls, replying messages very late till it gets to a point when they no longer communicate.

Ulterior motives

It is very common for people to get into relationships for reasons different from sharing their love energy. Some get in for money, sanctuary, to have children, and so many other things. Once these purposes have been achieved, their partner seems to be of no use anymore. It is tough to be in love with someone who no longer loves you, but it is far worse to be loved by someone you are no longer in love with.

Routine relationships

When all the things you do in your relationship become routine, it makes being with your partner like less exciting, which is not good for any relationship. Things you do in your relationship should be spontaneous, making every moment a thrilling one. It riles me to know that some couples have timetables. The love will deteriorate instantly. Having identified some of the things that affect love energy adversely in relationships, the next thing to address will be how to navigate your relationship without conflicts.

Self-love: You cannot love another person in a relationship unless you love yourself first, and the explanation is clear; you can't give what you don't have. You have to exhibit an unconditional love for yourself to rekindle the fire in your relationship. You need to take care of yourself. It would be best if you considered your individual needs, expectations, desires, and preferences. Only then can you transfer the kind of love that makes them look forward to being with you every time.

Emotional space: There are times when you feel anger, resentment, and intolerance either caused by your partner or not. It is normal, but when it happens, you need to take things easy and be understanding, do not lash out on your partner. Instead, request for some space, deal with your emotions, and replace those feelings with respect, acceptance, appreciation, and understanding. Relationships can be hard, but when negativity surfaces, you need to give and require space. The space in question is not a physical space, it is more of an emotional break, and partners often need it when they want to make important decisions or when the relationship becomes overwhelming.

Avoid comparing your partner to other people: There are times when you feel that your partner is not doing enough, and you think other couples are better. It is often never the case; everyone tends to go through something. Making comparisons is negative energy that often leads to mind-games in a relationship.

Know what's on their mind, if you can: Sometimes, you might have questions about what you feel, notice, or suspect about your lover. Instead of pretending everything is alright while something is eating you up on the inside, you should ask your partner about it, but only if they are ready to talk. Do not pressure them into giving you an answer, cause it may not be a sincere one. Remember this; great relationships are based on clarity, not mind-reading. But, allow your energy to find it's tune with your partner's energy. Doing so will grow your intuition and allow you to act without being told to do so.

Lower your expectations: If your partner does not put in as much effort as you are in making your relationship work, don't let it worry you. Everyone has a different way of expressing their love. Lowering your expectations is does not mean not to have standards. Maybe you're comparing the way you show love to your partner. You may be looking the wrong way. Instead, communicate your love language and learn theirs. Understanding your partner's expression of love is extremely important.

Compatibility, not perfection: There are no perfect men or women in relationships, and your partner certainly has flaws and imperfections. You should not expect a perfect partner, after establishing compatibility, it is your task to make them perfect by giving them so much love that they have no choice but to give it back.

Stay healthy and maintain those good looks that got their attention in the first place: I am not a judgemental person. However, I have seen some people go from looking one way before entering a relationship or getting married, and different afterward. In some instances, both people in the relationship have fallen victim to this. And the dynamic of the relationship has changed; they are no longer attracted to each other. In some cases, couples dial down on their appearance and lose focus on their health because they both have grown comfortable around each other. Maybe it used to make you feel nervous for your significant other to see you in your pajamas or without makeup, but now that you've been together for a while, those instances no longer scare you. While that is good in some ways, it could lead to your partner feeling a loss of attraction towards you or vice versa. On the other hand, the lack of effort could be for a variety of different reasons. Daily life can be exhausting, and now that you're in a committed relationship, keeping up appearances is not high on your list of priorities. Avoid this from happening because not only will taking care of yourself benefit your partner, but it's even more critical for you to feel healthy and happy with your appearance.

As for your health, being healthy will not only benefit your partner but you too. You will be the initial beneficiary of your partner's health status. When you look fit and healthy, with all the curves and abs formed from hitting the gym, you will notice the unwavering attraction your partner will feel towards you. You will also feel self-confident because of the positive affirmations and remarks your partner will be showering on you.

Rekindling

In a relationship, love should consistently be rekindled. You must keep adding fuel to the fire. Search for ways to spice up your relationship, search for things that you and your partner will do to create memorable moments you can always talk about—in a profound moment of love, thinking stops. The rekindling is so intriguing, so tremendously powerful, and the rekindling is so intensely alive, that thinking stops. You fall in love again and again.

Going out on dates has always been the best way to rekindle the flame of love in relationships, and the list of places you can go to or things you can do are endless. At least once a week, it would help if you went on dates, only the two of you. If kids are in the equation, get them a babysitter or let them stay with a relative. You can go out to a fancy restaurant (one of your budgets can afford), or watch a movie together. You could attend sporting events, go to concerts, or watch a play. There are countless places you could go, and part of the fun could be in taking turns picking a new place for your date night each week. Make sure to put in extra effort to look good for your partner. Wear something you don't wear every day and try to make this night of the week a special occasion. Act like the relationship is still new. You could try to remember and revisit all of the places you and your significant other would go when you were first dating, or you could pretend that you are brand new to the scene and find new places to call your favorites. During your date nights, try your best not to talk about the kids, money, or problems in your relationship. Forget your responsibilities or even who you are outside of the evening. Just have fun, talk about your interests, your hobbies, and your dreams. This can be a chance for you to rediscover each other. You may have forgotten all of the things that made you and your partner attracted to one another.

Appreciation

Always show your partner that you notice and appreciate all the little or unique things they do for you. However, it's easy to get stuck in everyday routines like going to work, cooking, cleaning, and shower, only to go to sleep and wake up and do the same thing all over again, day in and day out. Routines can deflate all the things and the people you should be thankful for. You almost become robotic, and you forget to thank your partner for taking out the trash, cooking, cleaning, doing laundry, and working hard for the family. A love note is a romantic way to express love, not in a text message, email, or social media post but in a genuine pen-on-paper love note. You can hand-deliver the love note to your significant other, mail it, or strategically put it in a place where they will find it and read it privately. A few suggestions on where you can place it will be to tuck it in their lunch box, taped to the steering wheel of their car, or propped against the bathroom mirror.

Surprises

Who doesn't like surprises? You can brighten your partner's day by doing something thoughtful, beautiful, and caring for them without them asking for it. Simple ways to pull a random act of kindness are to surprise your loved one with lunch, massages, doing a favor, gifts, cooking your loved one's favorite food or dessert, and so on. Learn and understand your partner's love language.

In summary, love is a great and powerful form of energy, and it is the one we often experience and share amongst ourselves in the form of relationships. There are also other negative emotional energies waiting to replace love. And so, allow positivity to guide your love energy. It is, therefore, your duty to rekindle this flame with your partner all the time. If you can achieve this, you will gain control of an aspect of your life that can change it for the better.

8

SELF-IMPROVEMENT I: CHANGE YOUR HABITS, CHANGE YOUR LIFE

"Your struggle has an expiration date."

P eople usually know that they struggle with issues about their lives when there is chakra imbalance or a distorted flow of energy. The physical interpretation is where they often miss it because, according to nature, you can't sow rice and get wheat.

Identifying bad habits

The first step to get you started on healthy habits is to recognize any potentially harmful behaviors you practice. These habits will bring down your levels of efficiency, satisfaction, or wellbeing. Its essential to acknowledge any bad habits you've got so you can remove them from your life and avoid having them become part of your routine. You may not even know you practice bad habits. That's why its essential to think about yourself, and you might also get ideas about what some potentially bad habits you may practice.

Avoid procrastination

A friend of mine once said that procrastination would be the death of us all. Maybe the world and humanity have not faced extinction-level threats, but recurrent events like the pandemics show what delayed action can cause on global scales. We're all tempted to procrastinate from time to time. When your habits are so small that it requires minimal effort, you become less likely to execute them.

Avoid overreacting

Overreacting doesn't get us anywhere. When you turn every little thing into a big deal, you'll cause unnecessary stress to yourself and those around you. It is critical not to be able to view your life as though it were a reality show. Instead, you have to respond to situations with precision. We tend to exaggerate things for other people's attention, but this tends to bring tension and unhappiness to those involved in the bad habit. Understanding to avoid overreacting will help you become a more reliable person and respond to circumstances more constructively.

Avoid perfectionism

Perfect is my least favorite word; it shouldn't exist. It's always great, of course, to wish to improve yourself. It would be best if you recognized that you have weaknesses you can work on, goals you can advance towards achieving, as well as knowledge you also need gain. You cannot get too fascinated with perfectionism, though. If you do, when you make mistakes, you will not be able to admit that. The reality is that everybody is making mistakes. You won't be good at all without first conducting practice. It takes time to get yourself improved and develop. You are your own harshest judge because you're a perfectionist. It can hurt not being respectful and patient of yourself.

"Every brick they threw at me, I used to stand on."

Replace bad habits with good habits

When you take out all your bad habits, you need to replace them with some good ones. In general, adding new patterns to your life is always good, as it will help you grow. You may also learn more about yourself and what you like. You can start a new habit to achieve your target, or you may want to add something special to your day. Whatever your reason for wanting to bring healthy habits into action, there are plenty of things you can try to apply to your life.

Improving your skills and deliberate practice

To change your life, you need to improve your skills until you reach a mastery level. Luckily, it's easier than ever to learn a new skill or improve an established one. With the Internet, we've got access to all the information in the world. We can learn whatever we want, often for little or no cost to us. We can purchase millions of Amazon books for a couple of bucks each, or stream millions of YouTube videos for free. There's no end on what we can learn. However, with so much information available, it's straightforward to get lost by switching from one skill to another without tangible results. That's why you must commit to mastering a few critical skills and be honest enough to recognize what needs work.

Deliberate practice is when you practice with a goal in mind. Deliberate practice is what differentiates someone who practices tennis for 15 years and becomes one of the top players from someone who plays tennis for 15 years as a hobby. While the first type of person keeps improving their game year after year, the second person only improves their game during the first few years of practice before getting stuck on a plateau for years on end.

9

SELF-IMPROVEMENT II: ENHANCE YOUR VIRTUES

"Two things define you: your patience when you have nothing and your attitude when you have everything." – Karma.

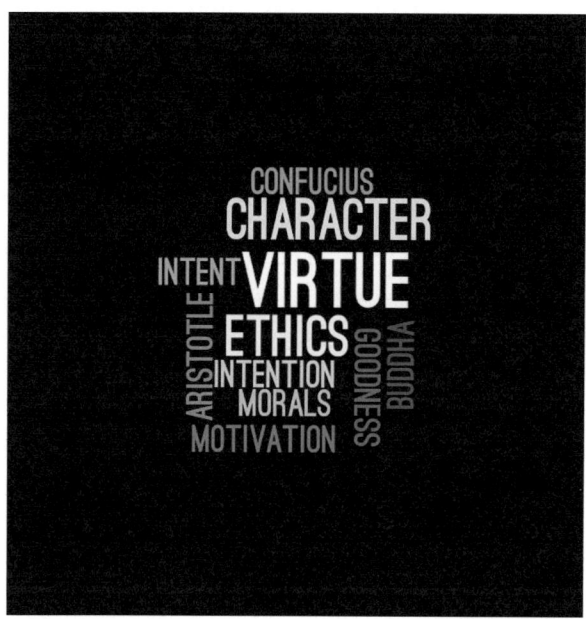

To change your life, you must also learn to be a better person, and maximizing your life requires external and internal changes. Although you can schedule your time correctly and start implementing good habits, it won't have as much effect if you don't change the person you are. Its essential to be positive, as this can have a considerable impact on how you feel. Being a better person is more than just being kind to others. It involves kindness to both yourself and others. Its essential to treat yourself well to practice positivity and have a greater appreciation for yourself. Practicing self-compassion is vital for you to be happy, and you can't treat others well until you learn how to treat yourself well. Patience is also crucial to learn. You must be patient with yourself, as everything will take time.

"People may destroy your image, stain your personality but they can't take away your good deeds because no matter how they describe you, you will still be admired by those who know you better."

Kindness and compassion

Kindness and compassion are important to self-improvement and an increase in positivity. You may practice both kindness and compassion towards yourself and others, helping you to be happier. When you learn to treat yourself better, you'll understand how to treat others better. You can spread more joy and positivity by living a life full of kindness and compassion. Kindness is usually the easiest to achieve because it does not take much to be kind. Using your manners is a great way to treat others with kindness. By merely thanking others for what they do, you can make someone's day better. It's always nice to know when what you do is appreciated. We often forget to thank others, and kindness overall may be something that is neglected. It's essential to take a few moments to make others' days brighter. You may also smile at others. Don't forget that strangers are people, too. It may mean volunteering somewhere or just removing some of the trash you see. And, through any spontaneous acts of kindness, you will make the world a happier place. You can visit a nursing home, send cards to the army, or thank someone for their work. You might consider paying in line for the person behind you or letting people line ahead of you.

Patience

Patience is essential to life, as there will be certain moments when you have to wait. Sometimes, you may have to wait for the others. When you want something so, and it seems your effort won't pay off, you've got to keep going and wait for your hard work to pay off. It is important to exercise patience in all aspects of your life. Patience will make you a much better person, and you're going to be happier about that. These days, almost everything has to be done instantly. We can have instant gratification with technology. You can instantly search for information on your phone and get it right away. If something takes more than a few moments, we'll start to panic. Through exercising flexibility, you can concentrate your efforts more than you need to do it immediately. Patience is the best remedy for every issue you face. Allow yourself the time to breathe, focus, and plan. Another critical thing to understand is that it is challenging to jump from little things to big things. It just takes time and patience. In summary, find patience in every you do in life.

Understanding

To be more understanding is a great ability to learn. If you understand, that doesn't mean you are endorsing any mistakes. You're not in agreement for anything. It is a smart way to combat perfectionism and to cut yourself a little slack. You're not always going to be okay, and nobody else is. It'sIt's important to remember that although you should always try to improve yourself and work hard, you also need to understand that there are times when it's okay to cut yourself a little loose. The highest activity anyone can attain is learning for understanding because to understand is to be free. Once you are mentally free, you can unlock several positive emotions. Such as appreciation, joy, love, passion, excitement, and freedom. Understanding is also the nature of love. Understanding someone suffering is the best gift you can give another person. Understanding is love's other name. If you don't understand, you can't love.

10

SELF-IMPROVEMENT III: DESIRE, GOALS AND PLANS

"Stop fearing what can be lost and start anticipating what can be gained."

Desires and goals work hand-in-hand to make your life be as you envisioned it. We often set goals to answer questions like what are your New Year's resolutions. What are your goals? What are you working towards, and how are you going to make yourself better? What is the purpose of your life, and what do you want to achieve? There are so many other ways in life with which you ask what you want. At times it can be quite stressful, as you may not even know what you want. You can compare yourself with others and feel you aren't doing enough.

It is crucial, though, that you set goals that you can achieve. At least one target towards which you will always be working. It's important to understand the types of goals you can set so that you don't limit yourself and achieve your full potential. After that, you have to develop a plan to achieve those goals and how you're going to make them. It's also essential to set priorities so that you don't overwhelm yourself and focus on what matters to you.

Prioritizing your goals

Now that you have a list of your goals, it's essential to know which ones you'd like to focus on. You may also set a few goals for this year and several long-term goals. It is also possible to set a few goals now that will help you reach longer-term objectives. Knowing that you're concentrating on goals, you're going to be able to pick the most important ones. Focusing on goals that you genuinely respect and feel passionate about will make it easier for you to be more inspired. When you want to concentrate on goals that you're not particularly excited about, you're not as likely to genuinely focus on them and give them your full effort. Prioritizing your goals will minimize stress, save time, and boost productivity. Make a to-do list with everything from routine tasks to important goals. Always remember, the best way to get some done is to begin.

Planning

Now that you know which goals you would like to work towards, you need an execution plan. How will you achieve all of your goals? Can you break it down? Is there a way to fine-tune your goals to make them even better or easier to achieve? You must consider all of these questions when planning out your goals, and there are a few steps you must take. It helps to be able to write down your goals, and it can also help to have another person to assist you with your goals. As the saying goes, a goal without a plan is just a wish. Even if your plan doesn't work, do your best not to change the goal but change the plan. When you are planning, start by making a simple list. Write down everything. Decide how long each thing may take. Schedule the when, and lastly, take a deep breath.

11

SELF-IMPROVEMENT IV: SELF-CARE

"Be more selfish. If you are a giver, always looking out for others, always feeling drained because you break yourself so others can stay together, take a break from it. Add value to your life first. Add self-love and peace to your life first."

To live your best life, and to be true to yourself is more than merely accomplishing all your goals. Enjoying your life is an absolute must. What is the point, after all, if you aren't even happy? There are a few ways you can help yourself make the most of your life. Self-care is going to make your ambitions look worth it all. You will be more optimistic and have a higher respect for life. Enjoying your life will give you a better picture of what matters to you and what life is all about.

Living your passion

Your life should be full of passion, happiness, and joy. We often try to force ourselves to carry things we don't like. We do what we think we should do because of how we are programmed. Or we follow someone else's course. That perspective or output of energy won't get you far, though. You have to support yourself because you are going to be there everywhere you go. Learn to spend time doing what you want and not what other people want. Eliminate what you don't want from your routine. The change will have a significant impact on you, and you're going to be much happier. You can change anything. Maybe you don't like going to the gym, and it doesn't suit you, but because you want to exercise and stay in shape, you feel like you must. So many other options do exist. You can go running, biking, swimming, joining a fitness class, or working from home. Think of your everyday routine, and about something you don't particularly like. How do you make the transition to be more enjoyable? There are many ways you can make your day more comfortable, and for you, this is an easy solution.

Gratitude

Taking a bit of time to practice gratitude every day can be of significant help to you. It is incredibly important to be grateful, thankful, and appreciative of all that life provides. It's hard not to be a positive person when you practice gratitude. Instead of what you want, you will be able to concentrate on what you have, which can significantly affect you. Finding the positive traits of people in your life, and finding positivity in all that happens will be more comfortable.

Practicing gratitude is relatively easy; it's free, fast, and can even be fun. It can make a big difference just a few minutes a day, and there are many ways to practice gratitude. For doing so, you will be a much more optimistic person, you will feel better about your life, and you will also be much more inspired. You can always choose; however, you wish to practice gratitude. You may switch it up every day because there are so many ways to do so. You have several choices to make, and there has to be at least one that works for you. You can express your gratitude by telling people how much you love them and how much you appreciate them. More often, smile, particularly at strangers; they are people also! Practice random acts of kindness with nothing to expect in return. Only call up friends and relatives to say hello. Volunteer for the causes for which you have passion. Contact those you haven't been talking to in a while. A perfect way to show appreciation is also to share time with others. Try to appreciate your time with them.

12

SELF-IMPROVEMENT V: SORTING YOUR FINANCES

"The best time to plant a tree was 20 years ago. The second best time is now."

Y ou can't talk about changing your life without taking about your finances because one very common and direct way to assess someone's life is from his or her finances. This also ties into that 'attitude of gratitude' that is always being discussed. Want to enjoy greater abundance? Then it would be best if you practiced appreciating the abundance already in your life. When you focus on positives, you move away from the negative energy, which could hinder your manifestation process. Your finances are not the conventional "Get rich in a number of steps" you see everywhere; it is more of creating and following a path towards financial freedom. Financially free people do not necessarily earn up to seven figures, but what is familiar to such people is that they are not in debt, and by debt, I mean the ones people don't get rid of quickly. They also have enough to sustain them and remain till their next paycheck or income, allowing them the luxury to set and achieve other financial goals for themselves other than simply living by. Be generous! Know that you already have everything you need and that the universe will see to the rest. When you find yourself dwelling on the subject of money, remind yourself of that all-important mantra: give-away to receive.

The problem

When a person lacks financial knowledge, they are more likely to con-centrate only on buying whatever they feel they need right now, till the money runs out. People live day by day in this situation, hoping that there will be some money to cover tomorrow's expenses. They typically rely too much on their job as their primary source of income, or their only source. However, if finance troubles are something you struggle with, you need to remember this: what we give our attention to grows. Focus on your lack of money or your money worries, and this is what you'll attract more of. An even more prevalent character flaw cultivated by many peo-ple is to over-spend and pay with borrowed money. The use of credit cards without financial education causes individuals to fall deeper into debt. People are putting themselves in a very precarious financial role in this case. Imagine what would happen if their work or source of income were lost today. They'd face some frightening times, especially if they have families. Although this scenario is more common in developing countries, it is not confined to underdeveloped nations. Financial reports show that developed economies around the world are experiencing it as well. The reason is that it has nothing to do with how much money a person earns, the kind of job they have, their bank interest rates, or the type of economy they live in. It doesn't even depend on whether they have a college degree or not. The reason is the lack of financial education, and a subject barely taught in schools.

The consequence

A financial word that is eating our society to its core is "Debt." You can't talk to five college students, or ten people in general without hearing something about Loan and Credit card. It is rampant and beginning to be a norm for people to be in debt from a very young age, which they could avoid. A Loan scenario could be someone who has a business plan that needs immediate execution. This person has saved a lot of money but still do not have enough to execute fully. This person may have saved enough for implementation but fears the opportunity may be lost and so needs a booster to start the business immediately. However, what Loan looks like nowadays is a scenario of someone at a shopping mall with credit card privileges in the guise of unlimited purchasing power, until the last purchase is declined. Because people know so little of their finances and the magnitude with which each financial decision they make affects every aspect of their finance, they end up making the worst decisions as they are usually the most appealing.

Why you should fix your finances

"Money can't buy happiness, but it sure makes it a lot easier to live with misery."

So, before we go further, there are two situations you don't want to be in by the end of the month, and they are; to be in debt or to not be in debt, but with a zero account balance. These two situations are terrible, and they stick when they occur because they possess features that make it difficult for victims of these situations to overcome them. If you ask the set of people in debt why they are still owing, the excuses are usually similar. You hear things like "I don't make enough money," "The interest rate is too high," "I couldn't pay it off even if I tried," "I don't have time to focus on it," "Everyone has debt," etc. and it is the same for the "break-even" category of people. Here is what happens next, nine out of ten of such people end up seeing vices and other criminal acts as the only way out while the other one percent give up and let the society toss them wherever it wills, either way, there is no happy ending for these people. Unless you are a wealthy prince or princess or have wealthy parents working endlessly for the future of their children, there is a chance that you will end up in any of the categories of people described here if you do not fix your finances.

The fix

The fix is a simple combo of financial education and taking actions to back up what you learned. Financial literacy will help you get the most out of your hard-earned income. Getting a good financial education is a must today. Because of the unstable economy in which we live, the price of a lack of financial literacy is far too high. Wherever you live in the world, learning about money and economics is an unfair advantage for those who don't. After learning the basics and what you need to do to fix your finance, the next thing is to take action, which involves making an updated financial statement, making a financial plan to repair your weak spots, and strictly following the plan. Along the way, your goals may change and may be lost in your financial plan, but when that happens, do not panic as it is an expected uncertainty, especially for first-timers. What you do at that point is to modify your steps or procedure but leave the goal undisturbed. Even if you do not meet the exact target, you will be close, and that is a victory to celebrate.

Financial statement

Your financial statements describe your lifestyle, but this time, with numbers; therefore, it is essential to know how to read them. One of the main reasons people have bad money habits is because they don't know how to prepare and understand financial statements. This is because we are not taught this vital skill in school unless you go to Business School, and very few students learn the importance of keeping personal financial statements. Once you learn how to prepare and read your financial statements, you will have an advantage over most people out there.

Your financial statement's goal is to provide a clear picture of the source and destination of your money. It refers to a specific period, usually a month. It will show you, within a month, how much money you earned, how you made it, what you spent it on, and how much you have left at the end of the period.

When you analyze this information, you will be able to track financial weaknesses such as bad spending habits; you will also have a better understanding of your current financial situation and find ways to be more efficient. Another significant benefit is that, once you determine your current financial situation, you will be able to set goals for what you would like your financial statements to look like. When you establish those goals, you will enter them in the form of a budget, and they will be your guide through the process of getting there.

Now, if you have a partner and both of you live together, it would be better to keep separate records of your transactions to make things easier. Then, by the end of each week, you can combine your separate documents into one financial statement. The reason is to be able to identify your weaknesses; however, if you have a different method of approach, it is your choice.

Items in the financial statement

Your financial statement can contain as many items as a spreadsheet can hold, and that is a lot, but most times, you can place those items into categories. For a simple or basic financial statement, most of your items will be grouped under income and expenses.

Income

There are three main sources of income, and they are: earned, passive, and Portfolio, which also includes capital gains. Your earned income is the one you work for, either as an employee or by being self-employed, that is, professionals, entrepreneurs, freelancers, etc. However, passive and Portfolio Incomes are generated per period by the assets you own, such as real estate, businesses, stocks, bonds, etc. Capital-gains income is the result of selling one of those assets.

Expenses

An expense is a monthly amount you pay on a liability, like a mortgage payment. They also include purchases of goods and services, donations, etc. when drafting a financial statement, it is common to split the list of expenses into three categories, which are Needs or Necessities, Lifestyle Expenses, and Charity.

Necessities

These are all the basic needs, things we can't do without that is, they are a must-have. Under this category, we have:

Housing: It includes the monthly payment for your mortgage and any other non-investment properties you own. In case you pay rent, list the monthly rent payment. Make sure to include all related housing costs and expenses such as insurance, maintenance, repairs, interests on the mortgage, etc. You should also include all the payments you make about services and utilities, such as electricity, water, gas, internet, phone bill, car note, etc.

Supplies & Groceries: This refers to all the expenses you make for basic needs, such as home supplies, groceries, cleaning and laundry, lawn & garden (if you have), postage, office supplies, etc.

Children Expenses:

This is for people that have children or are expectant, be sure to include all related expenses for each family member. The costs here include childcare, education, tuition, and supplies, private school, sports, child support, toys, religious training, etc.

Clothing: Includes all expenses related to clothes, accessories, and shoes, and they include purchases, alterations or repairs, etc. You will find items that represent luxuries like jewelry or high-end garments; they will be in the 'Lifestyle Expenses' section.

Medical expenses: This includes all the products and services you pay for, relating to maintaining good health. They cover medical services, prescriptions, medical insurance, medical co-payments, health club membership, health supplements, vitamins, massage, chiropractor visits, therapy, dental work, vision examinations, exercise equipment, etc.

Automobile and transportation: In this section, you include both the expenses related to having one or more vehicles and all the transportation costs you may incur as a car owner or not. The costs include a car loan, car lease, insurance, gas or servicing and maintenance, repairs, improvements, registration, and paperwork (license renewals), driver or chauffeur's salary (if you have one), taxi services (like Uber or Lyft), public transport, etc.

Credit cards and Loans: Here, you will include all the monthly installments you pay on other than your mortgage and car loan, and they include credit cards, personal loans, and student loans.

Taxes: This includes all your Federal and State taxes. Such as property tax on the houses you own for personal use (not the ones you rent out, those are considered in your Real Estate Statement), taxes for possessing vehicles, personal Income taxes (in case you have a balance when you do your annual tax file), etc.

Miscellaneous: Yes, it's a thing. We do have miscellaneous necessities; they include a diverse list of expenses that may not fit in the previous categories like interests, alimony, child support, bank fees, etc.

Lifestyle Expenses

These include all the "not so necessary" stuff we spend our money on. These are the kind of expenses where a lot of people spend more than necessary. It is vital to track these expenses for two main reasons. First, to realize how much of your income is going into unnecessary stuff that you could be directed somewhere else. Second, to determine precisely how much you can afford to spend on this category, then use this number to help you monitor your spending habits. This part of the financial statement is one of the most important ones in developing good financial habits.

Eating Out: This includes the expenses for dining outside of the home, including restaurants, coffee shops, to-go orders, etc. Usually, eating out represents a considerably higher expense than cooking at home; therefore, it is useful for budgeting purposes to have these concepts divided into separate categories like restaurant bills, purchased food to go, coffee shops. You can also include ordered foods via Uber Eats, etc.

Entertainment and fun: Here, you record all the expenses related to your hobbies and leisure activities in this section and they include streaming services (such as Netflix, Spotify, iTunes, etc.), cable TV, movies or theater, live events, bars and clubs, wine, liquor or beer, video games, hobby supplies or classes, collectibles, etc.

Personal Care: e.g. Examples of personal care are manicures, pedicures, haircuts, hairdos, make-up, waxing, etc.

Education, e.g., tuition, dues or subscriptions, books, and other resources. Education can be in the necessity section. Still, it is usually in lifestyle because of the flexible choices involved in education, like the type of school you choose and if you choose to attend online versus in-person.

Equipment and Furnishing: These include electronic equipment, tech devices, home appliances, computers, home office or workstation, furniture, art, sculptures, etc.

Travel and vacations: These are all the expenses you incur when traveling for leisure purposes. It would help if you did not list business travel expenses here unless your company or business does not cover them, and you have to pay for them yourself. Examples are vacation home, boats, hotels or lodging, restaurants, air or bus tickets, souvenirs, apparel, accessories, etc.

Gifts: Under gifts, you consider all the expenses you make in purchasing gifts for weddings or anniversaries, birthdays, holidays, or personal treats, etc.

Pets: Examples of expenses under pets are current and new pets, pet food, vet bills, accessories, clothing, furniture, etc.

Professional Services e.g. Examples of professional services are accounting or bookkeeping, tax planning, document preparation, wills and trusts, legal services, lawn care, car washes, etc.

Miscellaneous: The one we are all familiar with; this is where you record other expenses that won't fit in any of the previous categories. Additionally, you can always modify your financial statement by adding more rows as you need to.

Donations & Charity

Giving is in a universal law: "Give, and you shall receive." But how much you should give, and the reason for giving is up to you, and that is what determines whether it will be an expense or an investment to you.

Financial plan

Your financial plan is the new strategy you draw after assessing your financial statement. As an individual attempting to control your finances for the first time, your financial plan should not be complicated as in a business plan. What you need are some clearly stated goals you must achieve in terms of your finances, followed by the steps to take to achieve those financial goals. As with any other goal, your financial goal should be realistic. You will know you are lying when you say in the next three months, you would have cleared your debt of 40 thousand dollars and even become a millionaire, and you are in a job currently earning about $50k per year. While it may be feasible, it is rare and does not work for everybody. However, what will work for a majority will be to have paid up to 50 percent of your 40 thousand dollar debt from your $50K per year job. It is still stressful but more realistic compared to the first target.

Cash flow management

The thing more important than how much money you make is how much money you keep. Cash flow is likely the most significant concept in the world of personal finance. It is calculated by subtracting your expenses from income. If your expenses are more than your income, then your cash flow is negative and vice versa; therefore, your financial goal will be to maintain positive cash flow. If you're able to control your cash flow, you can manage your finances. Ideally, your cash flow is supposed to be more than half of what is left after deducting your necessities from your income. Here, you'll get some effective strategies that you can start to apply right now to take charge of your cash flow, and hence your financial life. There are only two ways to turn a negative cash flow into a positive one: to go from losing money to saving money by the end of the month; those two ways are either increasing your income or lowering your expenses. However, experience and lots of observation have shown that increasing income is not as effective as reducing expenses for positive cash flow.

Having a positive cash flow means that you are spending less than what you are earning, you are living within your means. This is one of the leading financial mantras you will hear from almost every personal finance guru, "live within your means." The truth is, nobody likes to live within their means. Who likes to be restricted in life? Everyone wants a life of abundance. Well, I think that to become wealthy and enjoy wealth, one must first become a good money administrator, even when starting with little. Or I should say, especially when starting with little money.

Developing good money habits when you don't have a lot of money is the best time to do it before you can spend and lose a lot. But anytime is a good time to educate yourself. Financial literacy will give you the skills to take control of your money now, so you can start growing your wealth and keep good habits along the way. Don't waste any more time and money; begin applying these lessons today.

Learning to live within your means is the foundation, the first step to achieving your goals. The next step is to increase your means to the point where you can live the life you want. Once you have control of your cash flow, it will be much easier to start growing your wealth. When you spend your money wisely and invest it efficiently, you will originate a spiral of wealth accumulation. Taking control of your money is the first phase of becoming as wealthy as you wish to be.

Increasing Your Income

It doesn't matter how you earn a living. Whether you are an employee, a self-employed person, a businessman, or an investor, there are always ways to increase your income. In cases where people can't figure out how to make more money, they only need to develop a bit of creativity and mix it with new information to find ways. Sometimes, they need someone to turn on the light on an idea in front of them so that they can see it.

If your current financial statement indicates that you need to increase your income to cover your monthly expenses or get out of debt, here are some ideas to generate more cash without giving up your current income. These ideas go from the obvious to the not so obvious.

Working overtime: This involves sacrificing a bit of your life. If your company allows you to work extra hours, do it, at least until you meet your goal. Remember it's a temporary situation. Working overtime at your current job is a better option over getting an extra job because, in most cases, you will get paid overtime rates; make sure it makes sense in terms of taxes. You can even talk to an accountant about it.

Getting a part-time job: If working overtime at your primary job is not the best option for you, or you would prefer to try a different activity in your spare time, consider looking for a side hustle. If you have thought of starting a business, but you have no experience working in the field you want to venture into, working part-time in that industry may be a good starting point. You will gain knowledge and some extra cash at the same time.

You can always get a job related to a hobby or passion you have, which might differ from your main profession. Think about fun jobs like bartending, modeling, work as an extra for films or TV, the list is endless, so try something you always wanted to do but never had the chance; you might find your next dream job. I mean, I became an author in my spare time.

Start a part-time business.

For most people, quitting their day job to start a business seems too risky and complicated, and completely understandable. Try following your entrepreneurial instincts without risking everything by keeping your day job and starting your business in your spare time. This way, you won't give up your income and risk all your savings simultaneously. Of course, the investment of time will be substantial, but everything worth it comes with a price tag.

It's important to remember that starting a business will require time and money. It doesn't have to be a lot of money, and it doesn't necessarily have to be your money. Just be aware that it might take some time before you start seeing profits.

Investments and monetization of assets: Investment involves taking a risk with your money and seeing what comes of it, but the potential profit and positive outlook will help you breathe. You can invest in cryptocurrencies and other stocks. Another way of earning more is by monetizing the thing you purchased originally under lifestyle expenses. For example, you could breed dogs; you could AirBnB your home or part of it. You can sell clothes you no longer wear or haven't worn. The possibilities are endless.

Spending less

Lowering your expenses is the second method of increasing your cash flow. The idea is to reduce those expenses to increase your cash flow and start growing a savings and an investment account. It would also help if you focused on paying off all bad debt; having credit power is extremely beneficial. Once you put your finances in order by getting rid of bad debt, building a savings fund, and controlling your cash flow, you will be able to expand your budget for those lifestyle expenses that you love. Always make sure you are in a good financial position before you go and spend on those lifestyle expenses.

Budgeting

Many successful businesses invest a lot of time and effort in setting up monthly and yearly budgets. And they work hard to stick to them, and that is the key. If you want financial success, then make and follow a budget. The task of setting up your budget is one of the most important habits you need to develop to achieve healthy finances. The primary strategy to control your expenses is to set a monthly budget for each expense category. Your budget will serve as a guide to monitor your spending behavior. It will help you make decisions on whether you can keep spending on a specific category or tighten up until your situation improves.

Controlling your expenses (No-spending policy)

This is more centered on lifestyle expenses. From your financial statement, you can make a list of things you can do without for some time. Other ways to control your expenses include:

Limiting your spending power by getting rid of all your credit cards except for one or two. Keep the ones with the best benefits, the lowest interest rate, and, ideally, no annual fees. Use them mainly for the benefits, not to purchase things on credit unless you need to. Always pay your balance off on time to avoid interest charges.

Applying for a personal loan with a lower interest rate is a great way to pay for your debt and cut costs. Even better, take out a car or home equity loan; this way, you will turn your unsecured debt into secured debt, charged with a lower interest rate. Just make sure to cancel all those credit cards and other credit lines, so the cycle of bad debt isn't repeated. A single loan with a lower interest rate will be easier to handle and less expensive than having multiple debts. Then focus on paying off that loan as soon as possible.

Resisting the urge for impulsive buying is another excellent method, if you don't need something specific, skip the visit to the mall. If you do need new clothes or a new laptop, shop for better deals or wait for a sale. Shop around for better deals on all kinds of goods and services, from your groceries to finding less expensive gas stations.

Delaying gratification and opting for the cheaper option. The "fake it till you make it" is one of the spending vices deteriorating our society. If you can't afford a vacation right now, be patient and wait instead of wasting the money you would have used to improve yourself. Clearing your debt should be a priority over spending on lifestyle expenses. Once you are debt-free, you will enjoy your vacation more. Always set up a budget for your trips and stick to it. Replace your car only when you have the right amount of cash flow and savings to do it. Buy a new home theatre or TV when the old one breaks down and always go for the cheaper option. It is not ideal to be following the expensive trends when you break even most month ends.

CONCLUSION

It might seem strange or uncomfortable at first when it comes to working with your energy. You may feel like you're in a different space like you're doing all wrong or confused about what you're doing. When you start working with your energy, you may not fully understand what that means or how it should look. It can be normal to want to rely on emotions to provide answers and to confirm that you are doing the right thing. I highly encourage you to ask questions, read, and study, but note that your energy is your own at the end of the day, and so are your ideas, opinions, and choices. Nobody can make that journey for you; you've got to make it for yourself. Choose what feels with you in honesty, and use it to help you deepen your energy experience. Be calm, but alert. Relaxed but ready. Smooth, but sharp. Humble but confident. I leave you with a promise. If you change your energy, you will change your life.

Made in the USA
Columbia, SC
30 May 2025

58280537R10042